SEP   2006

A School of
Dolphins

Heinemann Library
Chicago, Illinois

Richard and Louise Spilsbury

Originated by Dot Gradations Ltd
Printed in China by WKT

08 07 06 05 04
10 9 8 7 6 5 4 3 2

Library of Congress Cataloging-in-Publication Data
Spilsbury, Louise.
   A school of dolphins / Louise and Richard Spilsbury.
      p. cm. -- (Animal groups)
Summary: Describes the physical characteristics, behavior, habitat, and group life of dolphins.
Includes bibliographical references and index.
   ISBN 1-4034-4692-X (HC lib. bdg.) 1-4034-5420-5 (PB)
   1. Dolphins--Juvenile literature. [1. Dolphins.] I. Spilsbury,
Richard, 1963- II. Title. III. Series.
   QL737.C432S58 2004
   599.53--dc21
                              2003010344

Acknowledgments
The author and publishers are grateful to the following for permission to reproduce copyright material:

pp. 4, 10 NPL/Tom Walmsley; p. 6 Oxford Scientific Films/David Fleetham; p. 8 Corbis/George D. Lepp; p. 9 Oxford Scientific Films/Konrad Wothe; pp. 11, 22 Oxford Scientific Films/Gerard Soury; p. 12 NPL/Jeff Rotman; p. 14 NHPA/Norbert Wu; p. 15 FLPA/Foto Naturastock; p. 16 Still Pictures/Roland Seitre; p. 17 Oxford Scientific Films/Doug Allen; p. 18 NPL/Doc White; p. 19 Corbis; p. 20 FLPA/marinelane; p. 21 Image Bank; p. 23 FLPA/Minden Pictures/Flip Nicklin; p. 23 Oxford Scientific Films/Howard Hall; p. 24 Oxford Scientific Films/Des and Jen Bartlett; p. 25 FLPA/Nicklin/Minden; p. 26 NPL/Sue Flood; p. 27 Oxford Scientific Films/Will Darnell/Animals Animals; p. 28 NPL/Martha Holes.

Cover photograph of a school of dolphins reproduced with permission of FLPA/Minden Pictures/Flip Nicklin.

Every effort has been made to contact copyright holders of any material reproduced in this book. Any omissions will be rectified in subsequent printings if notice is given to the publisher.

Contents

Some words are shown in bold, **like this.** You can find out what they mean by looking in the glossary.

What Are Dolphins?

Some of the world's dolphins may look like fish as they dive and swim gracefully through the seas, but they are, in fact, small toothed **whales.** Like all whales, dolphins are **mammals**, not fish.

Dolphins have smooth, sleek skin and a torpedo-shaped body to help them swim easily through water. Most dolphins have a tail **fin** and a large, curved fin in the middle of their back. They also have two **flippers,** one on each side of their body. Dolphins have a long **snout,** which is sometimes called a beak. Inside this snout there may be up to 200 small teeth. Dolphins can be black, white, gray, yellow, brown, pink, or a mix of colors. Some are even spotted or striped!

This is a bottle-nosed dolphin. Dolphins are mammals and breathe air as we do. Dolphin mothers give birth to live young and feed their babies milk from their bodies.

Kinds of dolphins

There are about 32 different **species** of dolphins across the world. There are also six different species of porpoises, which are very similar to dolphins. Porpoises live in very similar ways to dolphins but they are smaller and faster and have different-shaped teeth.

Living in groups

Dolphins are among the most intelligent animals in the world. Each individual dolphin has its own personality, just like people. Some dolphins are shy; others are show-offs. Some dolphins are very bright; others are a little slower to learn. They may do some things on their own, but dolphins are **social** animals that spend most of their lives in groups. A group of dolphins is usually called a school or pod.

This is a group of common dolphins. When you see dolphins traveling, they are usually together in schools like this, or with a few members from the same group.

5

What Is a Dolphin School?

Schools of dolphins vary greatly in size. Bottle-nosed dolphin schools can be as small as a pair of dolphins or as large as 500. Most common dolphin schools have between 20 and 500 dolphins, but the largest can have tens of thousands of members out in the open ocean. River dolphins usually form small family groups of about five dolphins.

Groups within a school

Many large schools of dolphins contain **males** and **females** of all ages. Some dolphins form schools in other ways. Nursery groups contain mothers, their daughters, and all their **calves.** The adult males form separate **bachelor pods.** Some kinds of dolphins form groups according to age. For example, young adult dusky dolphins form schools separate from the older adults.

Dolphins may spend some time in small groups with five or six other dolphins from their school. Later, these small groups get together to feed or travel.

Why do dolphins live in a school?

Dolphins live in groups to help each other. Dolphins in a school help each other catch food, spot danger, and care for calves. Dolphins take care of sick or injured dolphins in their school and also seem to enjoy each other's company!

Dolphins need to swim to the surface regularly to breathe. If a dolphin is too tired, injured, or sick to do this, it may die. In a school of dolphins, there is usually someone on hand to give others a nudge up!

Who's who in a school?

In most schools of dolphins, some animals are more **dominant** than others. The larger or stronger male dolphins are usually dominant. Dominant males have a better chance of **mating** with female dolphins. They also get to swim at the top of the school, where it is easy for them to go to the surface to breathe.

Where Do Dolphins Live?

There are dolphins in all oceans of the world, from the cold waters near the North and South **Poles**, to warm **tropical** waters. Some kinds of dolphins live only in one part of the world. The New Zealand dolphin, as its name suggests, is found only in waters around New Zealand. Other dolphins, such as the bottle-nosed, are found in most of the world's oceans.

Some **species** of dolphins live in waters close to land. The five species of river dolphins live only in particular rivers and **estuaries**. Other kinds of dolphins spend all their lives far out at sea. Many dolphins live in different places at different times of the year. In the summer, southern right whale dolphins live in waters around Antarctica. In the winter, they move farther north, following the **shoals** of fish they like to eat.

This Pacific white-sided dolphin lives in the cold sea around British Columbia, Canada.

8

How do dolphins keep warm?

Mammals that live on land usually have hair on their bodies for warmth. **Whales** and dolphins have little or no hair, so how do they keep warm when swimming in cold or deep water? Dolphins have a thick layer of blubber, or fat, under their skin to keep them warm. The blubber stops them from losing their body warmth in the cold water around them.

How far do they travel?

Many dolphins live, swim, and feed in one particular area for most of the time. This is called their **home range.** Dolphin schools have ranges of different sizes. For example, spotted dolphins have a roughly circular home range, which is around 250 miles (400 kilometers) across. Within this range, they travel around 45 miles (70 kilometers) a day. They search for food, rest, play, and have young here.

These bottle-nosed dolphins are swimming in the warm tropical waters of the Caribbean.

9

How Do Dolphins Swim?

A dolphin's body is perfectly **adapted** to its life in the water. Its **streamlined** shape helps the dolphin move smoothly through water. The bones that make up a dolphin's skeleton are filled with fat and **oil.** This makes them a lot lighter than bones like ours, and helps to keep the dolphin from sinking. A dolphin uses the powerful **muscles** along its back to move its tail **flukes** up and down. This moves it forward through the water.

How fast can dolphins swim?

Most dolphins swim at about 6 to 9 miles (10 to 15 kilometers) per hour most of the time. People usually walk only at about 2 miles (3 kilometers) per hour! Dolphins can speed up to just over 30 miles (50 kilometers) an hour if they need to make a quick getaway.

This common dolphin is bow riding. Many dolphins do this. They use the force of water pushed in front of a moving boat to help them move along.

When a dolphin swims, it uses its **flippers** to steer, turn, slow down, and with the help of the flukes, to stop. Many dolphins also have a dorsal **fin** on their back. This helps keep a dolphin straight up in the water as it swims.

How long can dolphins stay underwater?

Most dolphins can stay underwater for about ten minutes at a time. Then they have to come back up to the surface to breathe. Dolphins breathe through their **blowhole.** When they swim underwater, they have to hold their breath. As they dive, a **muscular** skin flap covers the blowhole. This stops water from entering the blowhole and getting into their **lungs**, which would make them drown.

When dolphins are swimming along quickly, some types, such as these Atlantic spotted dolphins, leap right out of the water to take a quick breath of air before swimming on.

What Do Dolphins Eat?

All dolphins are **carnivores**—they eat other animals. Most kinds of dolphins eat fish and squid, although dolphins eat different kinds of foods, depending on where they live. Some dolphins eat a variety of foods, and others eat only one kind. River dolphins eat crab and clams from the river bed as well as fish. Risso's dolphins eat mainly squid. Some dolphins, such as the Pacific white-sided dolphin, usually eat fish that live in large **shoals**, such as anchovies and mackerel.

Bottle-nosed dolphins have about twenty pairs of small, cone-shaped teeth that they use to catch jellyfish, squid, and a wide variety of fish and shellfish.

How do dolphins eat?

A dolphin grabs and tears its **prey** with its many sharp teeth. All dolphins swallow their food whole or in large chunks because they do not have flat-topped teeth for chewing. Each day, dolphins eat up to one-third of their own body weight in food!

How Do Dolphins Find Food?

Most dolphins can see quite well, but it can be hard to see very far in rivers, seas, and oceans. It gets dark deep underwater, and shallow waters may be cloudy. Sound travels well in water, though, and dolphins have very good hearing, so they use sound rather than sight to find their prey.

What is echolocation?

Dolphins use **echolocation** to locate prey and to find their way around in dark waters. They send out a series of clicks and other sounds that bounce back from fish or other objects in the water. By listening to the echoes bounced back, a dolphin can tell the shape of an object and figure out what it is. The dolphin also can tell how far away it is and in which direction.

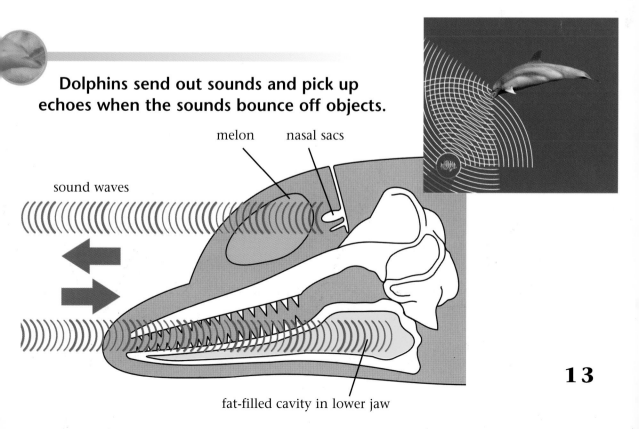

Dolphins send out sounds and pick up echoes when the sounds bounce off objects.

melon

nasal sacs

sound waves

fat-filled cavity in lower jaw

How do dolphins make echolocation sounds?

When dolphins make **echolocation** sounds, they do not open their mouths. They make the sounds inside their heads—a bit like when you hum. When the clicks echo back to the dolphin, they travel through its lower **jaw** and into its inner ear. The brain then figures out what the sounds mean.

Most dolphins have a large brow in the front of their head, although some have larger brows than others. A dolphin's rounded brow is called a melon because it is shaped like a melon fruit. In fact, a dolphin's melon is a swollen body part filled with fluid. It changes shape very slightly to aim the clicks a dolphin sends out to use for echolocation. A dolphin's melon can help it recognize tiny prey a few millimeters across!

Echolocation is important for river dolphins because most live in murky waters. They, and some other dolphins, move their head from side to side as they swim to send their echolocation clicks all around.

How Do Dolphin Schools Hunt?

Individual dolphins sometimes feed by themselves, but most often they hunt together in teams. Dolphins are very intelligent, and dolphin schools use a variety of hunting methods. Different kinds of dolphins may use different hunting skills. Methods also vary depending on what **prey** the dolphin school is trying to catch. Sometimes schools of different kinds of dolphins work together because many eat the same kinds of fish.

This Risso's dolphin is spy-hopping. Dolphins sometimes raise their heads up out of the water to look around for prey.

Hunting tactics

Groups of dolphins that live in the open ocean may hunt by swimming in circles around a **shoal** of fish. Gradually the circles they swim in become smaller and smaller, forcing the fish to form a tight shoal in the middle. Then the dolphins can swim through the tightly packed fish and eat.

Working together

Dolphins in a school take turns feeding. Some stay at the edge while others eat, making sure the shoal does not break up and the fish escape. Dolphins that hunt closer to shore often work together to chase fish into shallow water. Some dolphins keep the fish trapped in the shallow water while others feed.

Do dolphins ever team up with people?

In some parts of the world, dolphin schools work with humans as a way of getting food. Atlantic humpback dolphins have learned that if they chase large shoals of fish towards fishing nets near the shore, the fishers will throw them a share of the catch as a reward.

Large schools of common dolphins may work together to chase fish and force them to the surface of the water where it is impossible for them to escape.

These bottle-nosed dolphins have chased fish onto a muddy shore in the United States. The dolphins have to be careful not to go too far onto the beach. If they do, they may not be able to get back in the water.

How Do Dolphins Care for Their Young?

Most dolphins can have young at any time of the year. Different kinds of dolphins may carry babies for different lengths of time, but most baby dolphins are born nine to twelve months after parents have **mated**. Most adult **female** dolphins have a baby every two years.

Most dolphin babies are born just below the surface of the water. They are usually born tail first and can swim within minutes of being born. In many schools, other dolphins help the mother with the birth. Bottle-nosed dolphins may tug gently at the baby's tail as it comes out. They also protect the baby from any sharks that come by, attracted by the smell of the blood released during the birth.

Some kinds of dolphins, like these Atlantic spotted dolphins, swim together as a group to help a young dolphin up to the surface to take a breath!

What do dolphin babies look like?

Dolphin babies are called **calves**. Most calves look like smaller versions of their parents. Other kinds of young dolphins look different from how they will look as adults. For example, they may be a slightly different color, or they may not develop adult patterning until they are older. Most dolphin babies are about 3 feet (1 meter) long when they are born, but some **species** are smaller.

What do dolphin babies feed on?

Calves **suckle** milk from their mother underwater. Dolphin milk, like most **mammal** milk, is very rich in fat. It is a complete food for babies in the first part of their life, and it even provides the water they need. Calves only suckle for a few minutes at a time because they have to go to the surface regularly to breathe.

Spotted dolphin calves like the one in this picture are born gray all over. They only get their spots when they are older.

When do calves stop suckling?

Dolphin **calves suckle** for about a year to eighteen months. From about six months old, most calves begin to add some fish to their diet. Calves remain close to their mother's side for the first few years of life, even when they no longer need to suckle. Fathers usually return to **bachelor pods**, so they do not really help take care of the calves. Other dolphins in the mother's school help care for them.

How do young dolphins learn?

It is important for young dolphins to spend time with other members of their school. This close contact helps them get to know the other dolphins and learn how to behave. Young dolphins also learn how to swim, catch fish, **communicate**, and join in a hunt by watching and copying adults in their school.

A dolphin calf suckles from two nipples on its mother's belly. A mother's rich milk helps a baby grow quickly.

How does a dolphin school help raise calves?

When a mother needs to rest or wants to go off to feed without her calf, she usually leaves it with some young **female** dolphins from her school. This helps the mother, but it also teaches the young females. The babysitters learn how to care for calves so they will be better mothers when they grow up.

When is a dolphin grown up?

Dolphins, like many other animals, become adults when they are old enough to have young of their own. Different **species** of dolphins become adults at different ages. A bottle-nosed dolphin is an adult when it is around eight to ten years old.

When young Atlantic spotted dolphins swim with their mothers and other dolphins, they learn about life in a school.

21

How Do Dolphins Play and Rest?

Dolphins spend a large portion of every day playing. They have very sensitive skin and touch and nudge each other a lot when they chase and swim together. Dolphins often play with toys such as seaweed or feathers, which they throw to each other or toss around. They even surf in waves breaking near the shore. Playing improves **echolocation** and swimming skills and helps the dolphins feel like a group.

How do dolphins sleep?
Unlike humans, dolphins have to think about their breathing when they sleep. Each side of a dolphin's brain takes its turn to rest. While one side sleeps, the other side stays alert to make sure the dolphin breathes. Some dolphins sleep at the water's surface so their **blowhole** is always open to the air.

This bottle-nosed dolphin is taking a short nap for a few moments while it is swimming along.

22

Spinner dolphins can spin their body as many as seven times in a single leap. Many scientists believe they leap and spin together just for fun!

Sailors and divers often have seen dolphins playing with objects. These spotted dolphins are tossing and chasing a red scarf!

Do Dolphins Talk to Each Other?

When they hunt in teams, dolphins have to **communicate** to keep in touch with each other. They also communicate to warn each other of danger and to tell others food is nearby. Dolphins usually communicate using sound. Dolphins make lots of different sounds, including rattles, clicks, rasps, and whistles. They may make a kind of barking sound when they are angry, or squeak when they are being playful.

When a dolphin leaps high in the air like this, it is called breaching. **Males** often breach to attract the attention of a **female**.

What is body language?

Body language is when you use a part of your body to communicate, as we do when we frown, point, or wave. When dolphins are close enough to see each other, they also use body language. The most noticeable dolphin body language is breaching. This is when one dolphin leaps out of the water to make other dolphins notice it.

Male bottle-nosed dolphins twist their body into an S shape to tell the females they are ready to **mate.** Dolphins often show togetherness by swimming closely, side by side. The direction at which one dolphin swims towards another also has a special meaning. If a dolphins approaches quickly from the front or side, it may mean it is angry.

Dolphins often rub pectoral (back) **fins,** like this, when they meet. This is a sort of greeting, similar to a handshake or hug between two people.

Why do dolphins whistle?

In many **species,** each dolphin in a school has its own personal whistle sound, similar to having its own name. One dolphin may copy another dolphin's whistle to get its attention, just as you call out a friend's name. Sometimes many dolphins in a school whistle at once, repeating their whistle names again and again. This helps them keep in touch with each other.

Do Dolphins Fight?

Male dolphins fight over **female** dolphins when they are ready to **mate.** They also may fight over food. Before fighting, a dolphin tries to warn off another by using **displays.** Dolphins use displays to show they would win in a real fight. A male warning display might involve darting around, slapping its tail on the water's surface, and blowing water out of its **blowhole.** Another signal that they are ready to fight is a sharp, sideways head jerk with closed or open **jaws.**

If these displays do not scare off the other dolphin, the two fight. Dolphins fight by ramming or bumping each other with their hard noses, striking with their tail, or biting. They use their teeth to make scratches, called rake marks, on each other's skin.

This Risso's dolphin probably was scarred by other Risso's dolphins using their front teeth when fighting.

Killer **whales** and some kinds of shark are the only wild **predators** that hunt and eat dolphins. Even if dolphins are not killed when a shark or killer whale tries to catch them, they may die later from the wounds these predators can make.

The main reason dolphins have so few predators is that if a dolphin is attacked, the school works together to protect it. For example, if a shark moves in on a dolphin, the other dolphins in its school form a circle and work together to ram the shark until it leaves. Even great white sharks and killer whales are far less likely to attack dolphins when they are in large schools.

The maximum length of an adult killer whale is about 33 feet (10 meters). It has a powerful body that makes it an effective predator. Like dolphins, killer whales are **social** animals that often hunt in teams.

Do people harm dolphins?

People are a dolphin's biggest danger. Many fishing boats use huge nets that trap other animals, along with the sharks and fish they are meant to catch. When dolphins get caught in fishing nets, they often drown because they cannot get to the surface to breathe. Many people prefer to buy tuna with a "dolphin-friendly" label, which means the fish was caught on long lines and hooks that do not harm dolphins.

In some parts of the world, people hunt dolphins for food. **Pollution** in the oceans, such as old fishing nets, other garbage, and fuel **oil** leaked or dumped from ships, causes serious problems for sea animals.

In some places, fishers with vast nets are taking so many fish from the sea that there are not enough left for dolphins and other sea animals to eat. This is called overfishing.

Dolphin Facts

Do dolphins drink water?

Dolphins do not drink water. Sea water is very salty and not good to drink. Dolphins' main **prey**—fish and squid—contains large amounts of water so when dolphins eat them, they get all the water they need.

What is the largest school ever?

A school of common dolphins seen off the coast of New Zealand was 27 miles (44 kilometers) wide, and contained hundreds of thousands of dolphins.

Can dolphins smell?

Dolphins have little or no sense of smell. This is because their nostril hole—the **blowhole**—on the top of their head is **adapted** for breathing instead of smelling.

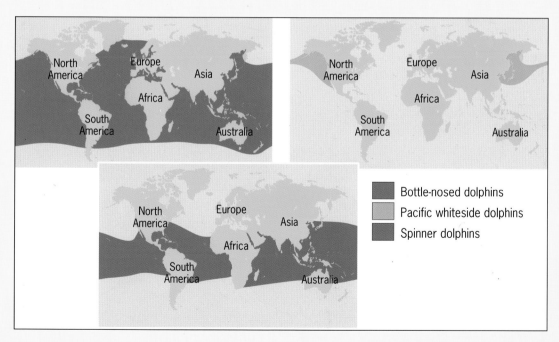

These maps show where bottle-nosed, Pacific whiteside, and spinner dolphins live.

Glossary

adapted when a living thing has special features that allow it to survive in its habitat

bachelor pod group of male dolphins

blowhole nostril hole on top of a dolphin's head

calf (more than one are called **calves**) baby dolphin still suckling from a mother

carnivore animal that eats other animals

communicate pass on information

display put on a show of actions or movements that sends a message to another animal

dominant leader of a group or most important member

echolocation finding objects or viewing surroundings using reflected sound

estuary part of river where it widens and meets the sea

female animal that, when grown up, can become a mother

fin flap or fold of skin that helps a fish swim

flipper front arm of a whale, used for steering through the water

fluke tail fin

home range area within a habitat that a group of animals lives in

jaw moving part of skull that opens and closes the mouth

lung part inside an animal's body that takes in oxygen

male animal that, when grown up, can become a father

mammal one of a group of animals that includes humans. All mammals feed their babies milk from their own bodies and have some hair.

mate produce young. After a male and female dolphin have mated, a baby begins to grow inside the female.

muscle/muscular part of the body that helps to make the bones and the rest of the body move. Muscular means full of muscles.

oil greasy substance that does not dissolve in water

Pole northernmost or southernmost point on Earth

pollution when something poisons or harms the natural world

predator animal that hunts or catches other animals to eat

prey animal that is hunted or caught for food by a predator

shoal group of fish

snout nose and mouth of an animal such as a dolphin or a dog

social living in a group

species group of living things that are similar and can produce healthy offspring together

streamlined smooth shape that moves through the water easily

suckle when a baby mammal drinks milk from its mother's body

tropical area around the Equator that has a very hot climate

whale mammal that spends its life in water. There are about 80 species of whales divided into two groups, toothed and baleen whales.

30

More Books to Read

Berger, Melvin and Gilda. *Is a Dolphin a Fish?* New York: Scholastic, 2002.

Gentle, Victor and Janet Perry. *Bottle-nosed Dolphins.* Milwaukee: Gareth Stevens, Inc., 2001.

Kendell, Patricia. *Dolphins.* Chicago: Raintree, 2002.

Laskey, Elizabeth. *Dolphins.* Chicago: Heinemann Library, 2003.

Schaefer, Lola M. *Dolphins.* Broomall, Penn.: Chelsea House Publishers, 2001.

Waxman, Laura Hamilton. *Diving Dolphins.* Minneapolis: Lerner Publishing Group, 2002.

Index